THE MAYOR OF BALTIMORE

& ANTHEM

53SP 11
August 2012

ISBN no. 978-0-9857577-0-0
Library of Congress Control no. 2012945166

53rdstatepress.org

Kristen Kosmas

THE MAYOR OF BALTIMORE

& ANTHEM

with an introduction by Andrew Horwitz

53rd State Press
Chicago, Illinois

INTRODUCTION

I have known Kristen Kosmas for probably just a little more than twenty years as I'm writing this. I'm not saying that to brag or to remind anybody of how old we both have become, just stating a fact, but an important one. Sometimes, I suppose, people write these kinds of introductions because someone asked them to but the introduction writer and the subject don't have any prior knowledge of each other. Sometimes they are asked to write these things because the subject is dead and the introduction writer spent a lot of time studying the subject's work and so is considered an expert. But I have known Kristen for years and am not even remotely an expert and she is still alive, so. This is not what I have come here to say.

I guess it is this: Kristen's writing changed my life. Or at least what I imagined writing about life could be and how writing about it could maybe, just maybe, change the way you live it and perceive it in the moment as you experience it and later upon reflection. This may embarrass her, I don't know. But it was in Seattle around 1992 or so and she performed her solo show (that I will not name here because I'm reasonably certain that it would embarrass her) at Room 608 (long gone now), and I saw it and I was transformed. I had never seen or heard anything like it, like her. Her cadences, her tone, her rhythm, her physicality, her stunning poetry and passion, her incisive ability to dissect pedestrian language and passing conversations into little slices of astonishing revelation, little windows into the profundity, tragedy and giddy nervous existential hilarity immanent in everyday life. I have never been the same as a writer or as a person.

As things do, as time goes, we lost touch and all of a sudden it was February 2006 and I found myself at Dixon Place, the old one in Ellie's loft on The Bowery, at a performance of *The Mayor Of Baltimore* and *Anthem*. It had been a long time and Kristen wasn't even in these plays, as she frequently is in her plays, and yet through these actors came her seemingly inimitable voice. It was a transporting, surprising and profoundly moving experience, to meet an old friend through the interpretation of others, to learn how much she'd grown and still stayed fantastically true. All those characters onstage, each unique unto themselves and yet still essentially variations of Kristen—but to abuse Whitman she is large, she contains multitudes.

I have re-read these plays, now, preparing for this essay. They are as strong on the page as performed because Kristen's voice is so singular and clear, because of her musicality and keen ear and fierce devotion to language in all its forms.

It is one of the beauties and frailties of printed text that I cannot completely or accurately convey how to make this work. And it is the beauty and frailty of theater that these words will respond to however you choose to embody them and, hopefully, provide your own unique way in. But as preparation, here is what I suggest, and this is only a suggestion: read them at least once through silently like a book of poems—imagine each phrase as a glittering glass bead. As you read, pay attention to the punctuation and imagine that it is not hesitation but wonderment, a moment of perplexing revelation, that draws you to end at a period or pause at a comma. Then prepare to read out loud, by yourself or with friends, colleagues, current and ex-lovers. Ground yourself, feet planted firmly on the ground, tilt your head lightly to one side, chin slightly elevated, hold your text in one hand and hold the other in the air about shoulder height and a foot from the body, palm inward, loose. Lean slightly forward; imagine your body solely dedicated to one purpose—the delivery of these words. Psychology is useless, it is all in the words—trust the language to show you how they are meant to be performed and embark on the text as if every utterance is a question of vital importance, as if you are strapped to the front of a locomotive of inevitability. And then, to misquote a friend of mine, tell us something true.

Andrew Horwitz, 2012

The Mayor of Baltimore

For Brooklyn. And everyone I ever loved there.

CHARACTERS

JOHN

MARGARET

TYRONE

PEARL

CHARLES

ANNELIE

SHELLY

NORMA

WES

VAL

ESTELLE

DAVE

THE VOICE OF CHARLES' MOM

SCENE

A small apartment in a forgotten American city. A store-bought party banner made of foil letters that says CONGRADULATIONS! [sic] is hanging center stage.

Charles' song and Annelie's lecture happen elsewhere. These places need not be represented.

A NOTE ON THE TEXT

Punctuation is not grammatical. It's for rhythm.

Italics, exclamation points, and descriptions such as "deflated", "depressed", and "hopeful" should be acknowledged but treated subtly.

Play it like music.

A NOTE ON THE STAGING

I like it when the play is staged simply. A series of static compositions. I like it when the architecture of the space determines the configuration of the scenes.

PRELUDE

In darkness. Voices, possibly on microphones.

JOHN: This is going to be a thing that will happen. It is going to happen and you are going to experience it.

MARGARET: I always think it's going to be fun. Every time, I think it's going to be fun. Ha!

TYRONE: I love you Pearl.

PEARL: I love you Charles.

CHARLES: I love you Annelie.

ANNELIE: I love you Oswald.

MARGARET: I love you John.

JOHN: I love you Shelly.

SHELLY: I love you twinset.

PEARL: I love you John.

TYRONE: I love you Tyrone.

MARGARET: I love you Shelly.

SHELLY: I love you corner store.

JOHN: I love you Margaret.

CHARLES: I love you Pearl.

ALL: *(overlapping)* I love you too. I love you too. I love you too. I love you too.

CHARLES' SONG

CHARLES plays the guitar and sings.

> None of these believers
> Got halos on
> They are just blendin' into the crowd
> And shinin' it on
>
> And none of my stories
> Are new it seems
> I never thought that this would be
> The thing that would comfort me
> I never thought that this would be
> The thing that would comfort me
>
> Yesterday I was frightened
> By a flock of birds
> I thought they were falling
> Like a handful of coins
> But birds don't fall
> And angels don't have wings
> Sometimes they have
> My very own face it seems
> Sometimes they have
> My very own face it seems

>
> None of these believers
> Needs a crown of thorns
> They can just blend into the crowd
> And shine it on
> They can just blend into the crowd
> And shine it on

THE VOICE OF CHARLES' MOM: Charles?

CHARLES: Yeah Mom?

THE VOICE OF CHARLES' MOM: What are you doing?

CHARLES: I'm getting ready for a party.

BLACKOUT.

PART ONE

JOHN and MARGARET stand in Margaret's barely furnished apartment. There's a little cart on wheels perhaps, with stuff for making drinks. Other than that, not much of anything.

JOHN: I don't think she's a lesbian, but the final scene of her movie does involve her deeply in the legs of another woman. Whatever that means.

MARGARET:

JOHN: So how do you feel? You should feel good right?

MARGARET: Yeah. I feel pretty good. I feel OK.

JOHN: Well I think you should feel good. I feel good for you.

MARGARET: Thanks.

SHELLY enters.

SHELLY: Hi Margaret.

MARGARET: Hey! Thanks for coming.

SHELLY: Of course. *(To JOHN)* Hello. Who are you?

MARGARET: Don't do that.

SHELLY: Well who is it? I don't recognize him. Is your name Roger?

MARGARET: It's so weird when you do that.

SHELLY: *(to JOHN)* Have we met before? Oh wait a minute. I remember. Second story of the Eiffel Tower, 1986, right?

JOHN: Right. So Margaret won!

SHELLY: I know. That's why we're here, right? We wouldn't be here if she lost would we?

MARGARET: I like to think that maybe we'd be here if I lost. Of course, the sign would say something different but—

JOHN: I'd be here!

SHELLY: What would it say?

MARGARET: Better luck next time?

SHELLY: So where is everybody? Who's coming? Is Annelie coming?

JOHN: She can't. She's giving a lecture.

LIGHTS UP on ANNELIE.

ANNELIE: Every time I hear sirens, I think of you.

LIGHTS OUT on ANNELIE.

CHARLES enters.

CHARLES: I'm here. I've got the window. Where do you want it?

MARGARET: Oh great! Right over there.

CHARLES goes to the place.

MARGARET: Yeah, flat like that. So we can look out of it from here. Perfect.

JOHN: Hey Charles.

CHARLES: Hey.

SHELLY: What's he doing?

MARGARET: He's putting up the window.

JOHN: You didn't invite him to the party?

MARGARET: I invited him to come over and put up the window. He can come to the party when he's done putting the window up, right Charles?

CHARLES: Yeah. Sure.

JOHN: Geez Margaret.

MARGARET: What?

JOHN:

SHELLY: We should put some music on. Can I play something?

MARGARET: Sure.

SOME MUSIC happens.

SHELLY dances to it and talks at the same time.

SHELLY: So I brought you a present Margaret. I got you a little something.

MARGARET: You didn't have to do that.

SHELLY: No. I wanted to. But I'm not quite ready to give it to you yet. I'll give it to you later.

SHELLY dances.

MARGARET: OK.

JOHN and MARGARET watch SHELLY dance.

CHARLES works on the window.

SOME TIME goes by like this.

. . .

MARGARET: So I went to the cancer hospital today. To pick up a pamphlet. About volunteering there? About how to be a volunteer there. I ran into my mother in the thrift store. The hospital thrift store. I picked out a sweater. The ladies who worked there told me I had good taste, said it was a tasteful sweater. My mother offered to buy it for me. She took out her wallet. Red fingernails flashing. I said, "I don't want that. I don't want you to do that for me." She waved her hands around like I was something crazy to be ignored. I said, "Mom. I have my own money. I won today. Did you even know that? That I won the election?" She said, white teeth gleaming, she said to the ladies, smiling, "She's my daughter. I'll buy it for her." They put it in a bag and gave it to me. "It's a present!" one of the ladies said. "Enjoy it!"

JOHN: I haven't seen my mother in years.

SHELLY stops dancing somewhere in here.

MARGARET: Then she says to me, my mother she says, "I used to know two men on the cancer ward. But they never call me anymore." I said, "Mom. You have to call them. They have cancer." She said, "I know. I know."

SHELLY: That's exactly what I'm talking about! *(Beat.)* You want your present now?

MARGARET: Sure.

SHELLY leaves to get the present.

JOHN goes to get a drink. As he's going:

JOHN: Do you think, going with this idea that we shouldn't take things personally, do you think also that we shouldn't take love personally? That if someone loves us, we're not supposed to feel good about that and feel good about ourselves that someone loves us? Is that ego, if we do that?

MARGARET: I dunno. Does someone love you?

JOHN comes back with the drink.

JOHN: I hope so. I'm thinking someone might. I'm sorry. That was rude. Did you want something? Do you want a drink?

MARGARET: No that's OK. I'm not ready yet.

TYRONE enters with a six-pack of Bud tallboys and a sandwich wrapped in white paper.

TYRONE: Hey you guys. Hey man. Hey Margaret. Congratulations! I brought a sandwich. Well, half a sandwich.

MARGARET: Thanks. Thanks for coming.

TYRONE: No man I'm happy for you. I'm glad to come. Thanks for inviting me. Thanks for winning! It gives me hope. At least now one of us will have some money. I'll just put the sandwich here. In case anyone wants some. Cool music.

TYRONE puts the sandwich somewhere and opens one of the beers. He puts his hand through the hole in the plastic thing and dangles the rest from his wrist.

SHELLY comes back without the present.

SHELLY: I'm sorry. I think I'm still not ready to give it to you yet.

MARGARET: That's OK. I didn't want any presents anyway.

SHELLY:

MARGARET:

JOHN: *(Sings.)*

> For she's a jolly good fellow
> For she's a jolly good fellow
> For she's a jolly good fe-eh-low

THE OTHERS join in.

ALL:

> Which nobody can deny!

JOHN, TYRONE, SHELLY, and CHARLES sing a couple of rounds of Jolly Good Fellow to MARGARET.

LIGHTS fade out on the party.

LIGHTS UP on ANNELIE.

ANNELIE: Can you—hear me?

THE AUDIENCE:

ANNELIE: So you can hear me?

THE AUDIENCE:

ANNELIE: What I'm interested in is—how—everyone—
always—does everything wrong. Especially the first time
around. But what I'm not interested in is—making a big
deal about it. What I want is—together with you here
is—to uncover, gently, like it was a baby, to uncover the
harrowing sweet—

*LIGHT lingers on ANNELIE for a moment while she doesn't go
forward with her speech. It's like a brief, collective amnesia.*

BLACKOUT on ANNELIE.

LIGHTS UP on the party. ALL still singing.

ALL: Nobody caaan denyyyyyyy!

MARGARET: Thanks you guys.

JOHN: Well we're just really happy for you Margaret.

PEARL enters.

PEARL: *(to JOHN)* Hi.

JOHN: Uh—

PEARL is wearing a costume.

PEARL: Oh no. *(To SHELLY)* Huh-Hi.

*PEARL is in underpants and a tank-top, gardening boots, and a
hat from the forties that fits close to the head.*

SHELLY: Hey Pearl.

A sort of cobbled together superhero ensemble.

24

PEARL: Oh great. This is great.

She might have temporary tattooed butterflies cascading all up and down an arm and a shoulder.

CHARLES: It's OK.

And possibly a few coming up out of one of the boots.

PEARL: *(to JOHN)* I thought this was a—John.

JOHN: I can see that.

Weirdly, she looks kind of sexy. But it's clear that's not what she was going for.

PEARL: I thought it was—Your birthday, I thought—

JOHN: Yeah, uhm—

SHELLY: Right, yeah, no, it isn't John's birthday, it's. A party. For Margaret. Margaret won today so we're. Celebrating!

TYRONE: Yeah Margaret's gonna have lots of power now.

PEARL: Oh.

MARGARET: I'm not going to have lots of power Tyrone.

PEARL: Wull

MARGARET: I'm not the mayor of *Baltimore* for godssake.

TYRONE: Well you're gonna have more power than I have. That's for sure.

MARGARET: I'm not going to have any *power*, Tyrone. It isn't a *power position*.

TYRONE: But it's a position. Doesn't any kind of position inherently imply power? More power, say, than the people who *don't* have the position? I mean right? Am I right?

PEARL: Well anyway congratulations.

MARGARET: Thanks.

PEARL: Yeah.

MARGARET: …I'm sorry. Have we? Met?

PEARL: …Are you serious?

MARGARET: Uuuhmm…

PEARL: Yes. We've met! We've *met*. We've met lots of times.

MARGARET: I'm sorry. I don't remember.

PEARL: I know! I know, you never remember. Jesus.

SHELLY: She meets so many people Pearl. She meets lots of people, sometimes she forgets.

PEARL: Oh I *know*. I *know* she does, she meets *lots* of people. Whereas I on the other hand, what? I haven't met anyone since—1974? Can I have a drink, please? Or something? Can I get a glass of wine or something?

JOHN: Yeah. Yeah sure.

JOHN goes to get PEARL a drink.

MARGARET: Do you want a sweater or something? Or some pants or?

PEARL: Can I just have something to sit on? Can I sit down somewhere please?

MARGARET goes to get PEARL something extremely impractical to sit on. Something too small and not made for sitting. Coming back with the thing:

MARGARET: I'm sorry. I don't have that much furniture.

TYRONE: Yet. *(As in: She will soon. Now that she's going to have lots of power and money.)*

PEARL: No this is perfect. This'll be great. *(She says hello to the thing.)* "Hello." *(She sits down on it.)*

JOHN comes back with a little clear plastic cup of red wine for PEARL.

JOHN: So what's your costume anyway?

PEARL: Rrright.

JOHN:

MARGARET: So does everyone know each other then? Tyrone? Do you know… ?

PEARL: Pearl! *Margaret.* My name is *Pearl*.

MARGARET: Okay.

PEARL: Yes, Tyrone and I know each other. Hello Tyrone.

TYRONE: Hey Pearl.

MARGARET: And you know Charles?

PEARL: Yes! Margaret! I know Charles! I know everyone *whom* you know. Hello Charles.

CHARLES: Hi Pearl.

TYRONE: *(Well into his beers.)* Oh my god! Margaret! I just remembered! I just remembered I had the craziest conversation with my sister on the telephone before I came over here. I was talking to my sister on the telephone before I came over here and I told her I was coming over here and I told her the reason I was coming over here and she asked me the craziest question about you. She said, "Is she the kind of person whose *outfits* match?" And I didn't know what to say! I mean. What does that *mean*? The "kind" of person? I mean, what is the *kind* of person whose *outfits* match? You know what I'm saying? I mean, I didn't know what to say to her. I mean, what does that *mean*?

MARGARET: What did you tell her?

TYRONE: *I* don't know. I didn't know *what* to tell her.

SHELLY: Looks like you coulda just said yes.

Apparently, MARGARET's outfit matches perfectly.

MARGARET: I think I'll have that drink now.

JOHN goes to get it. As he's going:

JOHN: You want a drink Charles? You want a beer or something?

CHARLES: No that's OK. Maybe when I'm done.

SHELLY: Are you sure you don't want a sweater?

PEARL: No. I'm fine.

TYRONE: I think she looks cool. I think you look kinda cool.

LIGHTS OUT on the party.

LIGHTS UP on ANNELIE.

ANNELIE: That is the important question. But does it matter? Does the important question even matter?

Maybe that is the even more important question, is whether or not the important question even matters. Whether then in fact it is important at all and what is important anyway and how do we know?

A comfortable chair. A good fork. A little help.

It's like we're losing certain muscles. The muscles that make the u, the muscles that bear children. How did I used to sit? What did I used to wonder? Who would love me. Now that I know that, now what do I think about? Want for? Wonder? Now I wonder what the love is, how the someone is doing it to me, now I want to look about it from all sides, see its relationship to household objects, things in nature, neurosis. I hate that word. Neurosis. Pretend I didn't say that.

I do I feel like I hate everything. Everything is an attempt at something. Some of everything succeeds at being what it is trying to be. Some of other things succeed at being things they are not trying to be. What am I supposed to make? Of that?

Airplanes. Helicopters. What can you say about them? I live in a city. There's a train. But it doesn't go everywhere. Which is some kind of a political... Or a poetical... But I am not so young anymore. They preserve things now. Have you noticed this? They preserve things in plastic and wear them like jewelry.

If you're a woman, have you noticed how, if you sit in a certain kind of chair, which at a certain height or angle or relation to your desk. And if you're doing something at your desk and you have to lean into it. And if maybe you're wearing a certain pair of pants which you bought when you were thinner and how you, you can still, fit into them but, they're not, they're a little bit tight on you, around the hips and thighs? And if you're working at your desk and you have to lean in, and you happen to, have your legs crossed, have you noticed how, the pressure? There's a certain pressure that, the seams of the pants are maybe applying to your, to the, to the area right around here. Have you noticed how strangely sexual that can feel sometimes? And have you wondered, Well then, I mean if *this* is sexual then, what is sexual? And why call it sexual? Have you ever wondered this?

Or like sometimes how you might just accidentally have to get something from the kitchen table which just happens to, come up to, right here on you, and how sometimes maybe you are putting something on the table or getting something from the table and you have to, again you have to, lean into it. And the corner of the table it, presses you here and you feel the same thing, the same, sexual, sensation, and then maybe you think it then, you think, That's strange. Sexual. What *does* that mean? But I don't know but I was just thinking about that.

BLACKOUT ON EVERYTHING. A baffling sound or series of sounds from the party. Crashing, falling, banging, breaking. Something like that.

JOHN: Whoa!

SHELLY: Oh my *god*!

PEARL: Goddammit—

TYRONE: Wow!

CHARLES: Are you all right?

PEARL: Yeah I'm fine. *Goddammit!*

TYRONE: That was awesome did you see that?

SHELLY: Shut up Tyrone.

TYRONE: What it was awesome.

SHELLY: I said shut up!

LIGHTS UP on ANNELIE.

ANNELIE: But words, right? I mean how to use them. Because how do I use them? What do I use them for? I mean, what good are they if they are only good for saying the same thing over and over? I love you. I love you. I don't like that. That was horrible. That was really good. There is that greenish light again. Everyone is always talking about that greenish light. That that that, love love, no no no, yes yes, etcetera. Sometimes I think, What? What else is there to say?

BLACKOUT on EVERYTHING.

A little silence.

Out of which:

PEARL: What happened to your eye?

CHARLES: Shiner.

PEARL: I can see *that*. Where'd you get it?

CHARLES: 'Smorning. Guy punched me.

LIGHTS UP on ANNELIE

ANNELIE: Or maybe it isn't about words. But you have to start somewhere.

I dreamed once that there was a way you could always be certain to be in the right place at the right time. And it was exciting at first. But then everyone realized that it wasn't enough. Because once you were in the right place at the right time, you still be had to be the right person, saying or doing the right thing.

There's so much responsibility that comes with being human. It can be so exhausting sometimes that you just want to die is all. Frankly, you just want to die. But who do you say that to?

And then maybe you'll find someone to say that to and then maybe you'll have sex with them. Press into them like they were your kitchen table. But then you'll realize that That's not love and then you'll wonder What is everything?

Once, I heard someone say, I think it was in a movie, "One must speak in a way that is right. Doesn't hurt." And I copied it down. Because I thought Right. I don't want to hurt. And I don't want to hurt. But lately. I don't know.

What is so wrong about hurting? And who do I think I am anyway?

No one can agree on what is natural. Have you noticed this? What is known and what is not known. No one can agree. What *is* everything, and what is nothing, and what is everything else.

LIGHTS OUT on ANNELIE.

INTERLUDE

More guests have arrived at the party.

Starts in darkness, then eventually, a pin-spot on NORMA. Pin-spot opens out slowly, or is added to, so that by the end of her story, we see the rest of the party. Possibly people in little islands of light.

NORMA: Actually, I don't think she was specifically in search of the women's bathroom, but rather... For any place where she could be alone. People who don't have delicate nervous systems don't understand this. This need to be alone sometimes when there is too much stimulation. But I have a delicate nervous system, so I understood what she was doing exactly. She drank too much. Because she was trying to make a little box around herself. A kind of... blurry... boundary. A buffer zone. She was trying to act like an extrovert. But it was coming off badly. Because really she is an introvert. And it is so awkward when you are attempting the wrong persona. So she got drunk and she went into the bathroom. And because she was drunk she fell asleep in there. And because she fell asleep in there, a long line started to form. So the proprietor went in to find out what was going on. And when he went in, he found her asleep in there. Seeing that she was helpless, the proprietor had his way with her. Which was mostly just kissing the already exposed parts of her skin and possibly... putting a hand on her breast. Just. Like this. *(She puts her own hand on one of her breasts.)* You know, nothing horrible. But still. Without her permission.

Anyway, when she woke up, she had a vague, sensual, pleasure-feeling in all of the places where the proprietor had touched her. She couldn't remember anything that had happened though. So she assumed it must have been her date. That he must have touched her and that they must have had a nice time. And so she couldn't wait to see him again.

WES: And then she said, "I have good news and I have bad news. The good news is that I'm not pregnant. But the bad news is that the baby I'm not pregnant with—isn't yours."

VAL: And what did you say?

WES: I said, "Well whose is it?"

VAL: And what did she say?

WES: She said, "You think I'm gonna tell you that? In any case, our vacation is over," she said. And then she left me. Right there.

VAL: Just like that?

WES: Just like that.

VAL: Wow.

CHARLES: Don't you think that somewhere, somewhere on this planet, there is someone who is worse than you are?

JOHN: No. No I don't.

CHARLES: Not someone who is worse off. But someone who is a worse person?

JOHN: Right. Yeah. No. I don't.

WES: Hey do you guys remember punk rock?

TYRONE: I do.

WES: Yeah. Me too. Right?

MARGARET: Everyone put these hats on. Everyone put these hats on.

PEARL & VAL: I already have a hat on.

MARGARET: Well take it off and put on one of these.

DAVE: And he says, "It is a privilege to hear from God. And it gives me great joy to relate my testimony to you. Having received instruction from God. Through divine revelation." !?!

NORMA: Dave, are you passionate?

DAVE: I like to think so.

NORMA: Do you like to play poker?

DAVE: …Yeah

NORMA: How do you feel about love, Dave?

DAVE: I feeeelll—

NORMA: Do you ever think: I *MUST* HAVE SOMEONE TO LOVE ME?!

DAVE: Yeah—

NORMA: I *MUST* HAVE SOMEONE TO LOVE ME *RIGHT NOW*?!

DAVE: Yeah I think that. I think that all the time.

NORMA: I would like to play poker with you Dave. I would lose. But I would like to play with you anyway.

ESTELLE: What happened to your eye?

CHARLES: Shiner.

ESTELLE: I can see that. How'd you get it?

CHARLES: Guy punched me.

WES's cell phone rings.

VAL: Meanwhile the snow. And all of our friends are leaving. And everyone needs a shower. And all that sadness. Piling up in the sink.

ESTELLE: Sadness? Piling up in the sink?

WES: Hello?

VAL: What?

ESTELLE: You said sadness. Piling up in the sink.

VAL and ESTELLE overlap with WES. Their conversation is dominant.

WES: Oh hey. Yeah I'm at a party can I call you back? Uhm… Margaret, and John, and Charles, and Tyrone, and Pearl, and Norma, and Val, and Estelle, and Dave, and uh… Shelly, and… *(looking out at the audience)* a buncha other people I don't know.

VAL: Oh I meant dishes. I meant to say dishes. Piling up in the sink.

ESTELLE: Yeah because sadness. Doesn't—

VAL: No of course not—

NORMA: It does at my house.

PEARL: *(Deflated.)* I'm cherryplum. You're so much *jacksier* than I am.

SHELLY: No. I'm just in style right now. You were in style before! I'm just in fashion. I'm not so jacksy.

PEARL: I'm cherryplum. I'm applefloss. You're glitterstorm! You're swirlingforth!

WES: Yeah, no, it's cool, I'll call you back. A'ight. Bye.

PEARL: *(Depressed.)* What am I wearing?

NORMA: You know what I don't get? Is contemporary Greek cinema.

ESTELLE: Contemporary? Greek? Cinema?

NORMA: Yeah. There's no dialogue. I don't get that.

CHARLES: Don't you think that *somewhere*, there is someone somewhere on this planet, who is worse than you?

SHELLY: No. I don't.

CHARLES: Not someone who is worse *off*. But someone who is a worse *person*.

SHELLY: Oh. Yeah. Definitely. Lots of people. Some of them are even in this room.

The conversations overlap a little more and more.

JOHN: *(Referring to the CONGRADULATIONS sign.)* You know why that's like that, right? It's because the Cowboy spelled it like that once, so they changed it so it would be right. No, that's how you spell it now. They've changed lots of

the rules so the Cowboy won't look stupid. *("The Cowboy"
refers to a recent American president. Who was, apparently, an
idiot.)*

TYRONE: Now *that's* what I'm talking about. Now that's
power.

SHELLY: That's exactly what I'm *talking* about!

ESTELLE: It's got to stop. I love it so much, but it's got to
stop. And I think: Who can make it stop? And I think: Who
the hell knows? And so I just pray. Every day. I just get
right down on my hands and knees and beg for mercy.

TYRONE: You know I think maybe *I* should be the mayor of
Baltimore.

SHELLY: Yeah right.

TYRONE: What?

SHELLY: Agh! GOD! *Je*sus! God*damnit*! God. Fucking.
Dammit. Agh!

SHELLY storms out of the room.

A big long silence.

WES: If you guys knew what I was thinking about right now,
it'd blow your minds.

MARGARET: Clichés are the new experiments. Did you
guys know that? I heard that somewhere.

VAL: I heard people want meaning again.

TYRONE: I heard top is the new bottom.

MARGARET: Pff. I don't think *that's* true.

ESTELLE: No but I mean seriously. Where are everyone's pants? Is it the economy? People can't afford pants?

SHELLY: Yes! Yes yes yes yes yes yes yes! That's what I'm *talking* about!

TYRONE: *How'd* you get it?

CHARLES: Guy punched me.

TYRONE: Someone you know?

CHARLES: Why would someone I know punch me in the face?

VAL: And it says "list of reasons to go on living"

CHARLES: No. I was coming to work this morning

VAL: and then it's blank.

CHARLES: and I heard this guy playing his guitar on the street.

VAL: There's nothing there. There's nothing on the list.

CHARLES: And I thought it sounded good. So I went over and I was about to throw my lunch money into his guitar case, which was there, opened, when he punched me in the eye. I said, "Hey. What'd you do that for?" And he said, "What are you doing?" And I said, "I thought you were a homeless." And he said, "Well I'm not. I'm in a band." And I said, "OK well. I didn't know." And he said, "OK well. Now you do."

SHELLY: When are we gonna learn *Spanish*?! What are we going to do about all this *garbage*?!

JOHN: Who said that?

TYRONE: You were gonna give him your lunch money?

JOHN: No I'm serious. Who just said that?

CHARLES: He sounded good.

WES: Hey man. Can I get one a those beers?

TYRONE: No. Has anybody seen my f'in sandwich?

NORMA: How do you say, "I want to touch you. With my fingertips. I want to start here and move all the way down and along the outside of your body. Then with my lips. Then with my teeth. I want to bite little bruises into your skin all along the edges, like seams." How do you say that?

VAL: I don't know how to say that.

NORMA: Try!

VAL: *(Says that in a foreign language.)*

TYRONE: I had a good morning.

CHARLES: Yeah?

TYRONE: Yeah I smelled this girl on the train. Smelled just like my first girlfriend from junior high. Jennifer. Her name was Jennifer.

MARGARET: I liked walking. Today. I liked just—getting up early and—leaving the apartment and just—walking around the corner.

JOHN: Yeah I know what you mean.

41

MARGARET: I think I'll do it again tomorrow.

JOHN: That's a good idea.

DAVE: And this guy starts singing, *(singing)* "Here comes the sun. Little darlin'. Here comes the sun and I say. It's all right. Dadadadadadadadadadadadadadaduhm."

NORMA: Oh I love that song!

DAVE: Yeah me too, and I perked up for a minute you know? Because I thought "It's true! Here does come the sun!" And isn't that all we're waiting for really? Is a little light? And a little truth? A little something we can believe in?

ESTELLE: I don't know what I'm waiting for.

MARGARET: Feeling nothing?

VAL: Feeling nothing? That's a goal?

A pause in the party. People move around. People get drinks and rearrange. Maybe someone kicks something across the floor. Not violent. Just out of curiosity. Or boredom.

PEARL: The window is looking good Charles.

CHARLES: Thanks.

PEARL: No. I mean it. Really.

CHARLES: Thanks.

. . .

CHARLES: Hey… Pearl?

PEARL: Yeah?

CHARLES: I've been meaning to tell you. I've been meaning to tell you... I think it's really, really sexy. How in love you are with your husband.

PEARL: ...You do?

CHARLES: Yeah. I do.

PEARL and CHARLES stare at each other for a long time. They want to make out.

NORMA: Well anyway. I'm sorry I was such a bitch the last time I saw you.

VAL: That's OK.

NORMA:

VAL: No really. It's OK.

ESTELLE: Yeah you were a real bitch the last time I saw you too.

• • •

SHELLY: So. Margaret. Do you uh. Do you want your present now?

MARGARET: Yeah! Sure!

SHELLY leaves to get the present.

BLACKOUT on the party.

LIGHTS UP on ANNELIE.

ANNELIE: I just want one word. That's all I want. Just one. Just one word. Just one word. That's all I want. That's all. Just one. That would be enough. Just one. Just enough. Just enough. That's all I want. Just enough. Just one. Enough. One. Enough.

BLACKOUT on ANNELIE.

PART TWO

SHELLY is back with the present. She and MARGARET and JOHN are looking at it. It is something not too small that lights up and hopefully blinks. It should be beautiful, whatever it is. It should have a whole moment to itself.

MARGARET: That's beautiful. Is that for me?

SHELLY: Yeah...

MARGARET: Thanks. Thank you.

SHELLY: Yeah, I don't know...

JOHN, MARGARET and SHELLY create a kind of stillness at the center of the party. EVERYONE ELSE is talking quietly, underneath, about this, or that, or whatever.

MARGARET: I dreamed about Mrs. Pinkerton again last night.

SHELLY: Oh no. No. I can't listen to a Mrs. Pinkerton dream right now.

MARGARET: But I had it.

SHELLY: I'm sure you had it but can we not talk about it right now?

JOHN: But she wants to talk about it Shelly. She needs to talk about it.

SHELLY: Why? The guilt? She needs to talk about the guilt that she feels right now? Why do you need to talk about the guilt?

JOHN: Shelly.

MARGARET: Because that's what I woke up feeling.

SHELLY: Yes but why talk about it?

MARGARET: Because what else can I do? It's what I'm thinking about.

SHELLY: OK but why are you thinking about *that*? Today? Of all days why do you have to think about *that*?

JOHN: Why do you think you still feel it? You were so young Margaret. What were you, like twelve?

MARGARET: No I wasn't *even* twelve.

SHELLY: OK all the more reason not to talk about it! Let's just make up a rule that we can't talk about anything that happened before we were twelve. We can't feel guilty about anything we did before we were twelve.

JOHN: But she feels it.

SHELLY: Well doesn't she feel anything else?! It's your big day for godssake. Give yourself a present. Give yourself a little reward: Forgive yourself for what you did to Mrs. Pinkerton's child when you were a pre-teen babysitter. I will never let children look after my children, I swear to god.

MARGARET: See? That. Right there. What you just did. I don't need that right now. I need the opposite of that.

SHELLY: You need the opposite of forgiving yourself?

MARGARET: What you just said about not letting children look after your children. It makes me feel bad.

JOHN: *(Hopeful.)* You're going to have children?

SHELLY: I'm just saying.

MARGARET: I don't know Shelly. I really don't understand you sometimes.

SHELLY: OK talk about it. Go ahead and talk about it. In fact, talk about it all night! Anyway, I'm leaving.

JOHN: Shelly.

SHELLY: Roger?

JOHN: John.

SHELLY: John.

EVERYONE ELSE sort of enters the conversation.

TYRONE: What's going on?

SHELLY: I can't handle it. I can't listen to this dream one more time. I'm happy for you Margaret. Really. I'm so happy you won but I can't—Bless your heart. You know? Bless your tiny, naive, Republican heart. Really but—

MARGARET: I'm not a Republican!

SHELLY: But you are. Margaret. Basically you are. When you look right down into it. And I'm happy for you, OK? But I can't do this anymore. It's like being glad for someone who's wanted a boyfriend for so long and then they finally get one but he beats the shit out of her. You know what I think about your dream? Is that you'll stop having it when you stop being evil.

MARGARET: I'm not evil!

TYRONE: Dude, don't say Republican at a party.

MARGARET: And I'm not a Republican!

CHARLES: I think maybe everybody doesn't give the Republicans maybe enough credit. Plato was a Republican.

SHELLY: And he was a fascist!

TYRONE: Wasn't he like, the *original* Republican?

CHARLES: *(to SHELLY)* If you see it that way.

NORMA: But he was also a genius.

CHARLES: *(still to SHELLY)* If you need to see it that way.

VAL: A fascist genius.

DAVE: Wait. Which one was Plato?

SHELLY: I don't "need" to see it that way! I can see it for how it is!

MARGARET: This party sucks.

JOHN: It's like having a telephone conversation with no telephone.

SHELLY: *(to MARGARET)* I mean don't you think that in some way it was Mrs. Pinkerton's own fault? For letting you look after her child when you were only a child yourself? Children are cruel, and curious by nature. Shouldn't Mrs. Pinkerton know this? Having once been a child herself, and then, having given *birth* to *four* of them?! I mean wasn't she ever paying attention to *any*thing, Mrs. Pinkerton? Except what big plastic cup she could hide her next gin and juice in?

JOHN: Shelly.

SHELLY: NO! It's exactly what I'm talking about! Do you have any idea what's going on out there? Do you have any idea that there are old men out there falling down in the streets out there and skinning the palms of their hands? They're getting infections! They don't have any shoes! There are Japanese *weeping* at their steering wheels. Tanning salons are doing a booming business. Undercover cops disguised as party clowns are setting up crack whores to get busted. And all of this is legal?!

JOHN: Many things which are legal are offensive Shelly.

SHELLY: Yes! Yes! The death penalty! Telemarketing! Web blogging. And this is the world? This is what we're going to call the world we're going to say it's OK like this? I can't do it anymore. I can't crawl around anymore in my underwear on the kitchen floor drinking all of the milk out of the carton in one sitting with the refrigerator door open and all the energy leaking out and wait for the night to be over. I have to *do* something! I have to do something *else*.

JOHN: But do you even have a lasso? Shelly? Do you have a lasso?

SHELLY: I don't need a lasso, *John*!

TYRONE: You were gonna give him your lunch money?

CHARLES: He sounded good. And there's so little feeling of the soul out there.

MARGARET: *(to SHELLY)* I went outside this morning. I

went out to the park and I looked at the swing set and I thought, "Poor swing. Nobody swings you." But instead of getting sad about it, I got on the swing and I swung it until I thought that was enough. I understand a little bit. But I wish you didn't feel like you needed to leave today. Or. I wish you had waited maybe until maybe tomorrow to tell us. Because I really was hoping for a nice party. I could have used that. I've worked really hard you know. And it hasn't been easy for me. I thought maybe you would maybe sing me a song.

SHELLY: You want me to sing you a song? OK. I'll sing you a song. In fact, I wrote this little song in the coffee shop today.

SHELLY sings:

> I hate it here
> I've got to get out of here
> I can't stay here
> Anymore
>
> I hate it here
> I can't be myself here
> It's ugly here
> And I can't think or feel here
>
> Except when I think negative things
> Or feel negative things
> And then I hate myself
> Because I'm even thinking these

Negative things about you
And that makes me think
A bunch of negative things
About me

And I'm tired of that
I'm so tired of that
I'm so tired of that
I'm so tired

Nothing ever grows here, here everything only dies
And you may say I'm only seeing
The dark, dark dark dark dark dark dark dark side

But that's what it is when I open my eyes
That is all I see
And I'm tired
From straining
From straining and straining and straining
To see the light
So I'm leaving here
I'm leaving here
Tonight

DAVE claps.

NOBODY ELSE claps.

DAVE stops clapping.

MARGARET: Why can't you use your imagination to make anything nice for us?

BLACKOUT on the party.

LIGHTS UP on ANNELIE.

ANNELIE: Um... I'm sorry. I forgot what I was going to say.

BLACKOUT on ANNELIE.

LIGHTS UP on the party.

CHARLES: Maybe this was a nice party Margaret. After all. Maybe this was just the party you needed.

MARGARET: Shut up Charles.

CHARLES: I'm just saying.

MARGARET: Shut up! I can't stand your infernal optimism! I'll have to kill you if you don't shut up!

CHARLES: OK but Margaret?

JOHN: Charles.

CHARLES: Way out beyond all that fuss and bother? Is a big, clear, bright blue sky.

VAL: Charles really you ought to stop it. It's embarrassing. You're not even a Buddhist.

CHARLES: I never said I was a Buddhist.

PEARL: *(Loving CHARLES.)* I wasn't happy with my previous future. Charles. I wasn't happy with my previous future.

SHELLY: I'm sorry. I have to go. I have to go now.

JOHN: So I guess nobody really does love me after all.

SHELLY: I don't have room for a sidekick. I'm sorry. Congratulations Margaret. Really I'm glad for you.

SHELLY leaves.

EVERYONE ELSE files out in an awkward rhythm. Little phrases like "OK well" and "taking the bus?" and "get my bag" and "ride with you?" are sort of almost heard as ALL depart.

MARGARET and JOHN stand there for a while.

Eventually:

MARGARET: I love you John.

JOHN: I know...

MARGARET: ... I know.

ANNELIE: The moon floating beyond the window. The stream they fountain made itself river and waved.

JOHN: I always wanted to be something once. *(As in: Like Shelly wants to be something now.)*

ANNELIE: Now, somewhere into dishes fell clattering.

JOHN: An oceanographer.

The following texts may overlap. I leave it to you.

ANNELIE: Red headed girl flung eclipse infrequent. Transposed and befallen rupture rhapsodic. Gradual Bloomington wind fall sky wave. Mufflehug capacitance on first impression, in the light airports anywhere. Cairo fast, Dante ambiguous, a moment later revolve for what purpose. Plaintive Croatia swear crochet April, washy daisy dainty to kiss remained antagonistic. Exclusive Eileen lamp shaded with here the insane, yourself with this herein after instinctual velocity. Opened his eyes there was also sky, and strike, sleep peacefully, and share kitchen.

JOHN: I can see that there are crimes. Loneliness. Humiliation. Amnesia persists in several categories. The soul, the mind, the genitals. It's all under serious attack. The teeth, the blood, the whole elaborate system of gods and monsters. The records-keeping department is in ill-repair. To say the least. Recipes have been lost. Family albums. Virginities. Senses of humor, and purpose. I can see this.

MARGARET: Is there something coming out of me? Is there something coming out of me, down there? Light? Is there light coming out of me? It feels like something's coming out of me.

ANNELIE: Aftermath Humphrey couch breakthrough himself hanging from there a conversation. Go up past I love you, scram archangel. Ricochet poured water into keepsake northwest music box, pursuant daybed let him come I say, let him come.

JOHN: The ocean is relaxing. Fish are relaxing. Waves are relaxing. The color blue is relaxing. Whales are a miracle. Coral. Starfish. Sand. Feels good on your feet. Wetsuits are funny. Flippers. The sound of breathing underwater. Bubbles. Boats. The manatee. The horizon. Sunken treasure. Myth of pirates. Eye patches and peg legs. Desert islands. Richard Dreyfus. Secret languages. Sunburn. Salty dogs. Journals fat with moisture. Puka shells. Yeah. I shoulda *done* that. I shoulda *done* that. With my life.

ANNELIE: Many observations from other things like sagging boardinghouse gravy Yankee narcissism ever departing from moonlit biometry daze. Dishes fell clattering again while the rest certainly take something what's wrong with—compassionate inconsequential porch Marseilles? Amputate curtsey, and Anabaptist frailty.

MARGARET'S SONG

MARGARET stands there and sings.

> Nothing compares to
> Tyco Brahe's humiliation
> Fortunately for him
> He didn't have
> To live through it
>
> Everyone thinks they know
> The shape of the stars and the sky
> Still everyone is asking
> How and when and why

He comes in the room half broken
And we are all choking on his air
Pretending he's not there
Pretending that's love

I've walked a mile in the sweaters
Of people with broken arms
I've walked a mile in the shoes
Of people with broken hearts
It's never gotten me far
It's never gotten me anywhere
It's never gotten me far
It's never gotten me anywhere

Nothing compares to
Tyco Brahe's humiliation
Fortunately for him
He didn't have to live through it

THE LIGHTS fade out.

The PRESENT from SHELLY blinks in the darkness.

EPILUDE

The AUDIENCE hears ANNELIE's voice.

ANNELIE: Margaret? Are you guys there still? Look out the window. I'm down on the street. I've brought you something. I'm sorry I'm so late. Look what I found. I'm sorry I'm so late but I've been out all night looking for something to bring you. I know you said you didn't want any presents but I couldn't resist. I really wanted to bring you something beautiful. I know beauty is the desperate concern of your soul. But there's almost nothing beautiful left. Were you aware of that? I think you probably were. I almost gave up but then at the very last minute I found this. And I mean I really found it. It wasn't in a shop or anything. It was just there, out, anyone could have taken it. But maybe no one recognized it. But anyway I wanted to give it to you. I hope you like it. Charles? Is anyone here still? Margaret? Congratulations. Are you guys awake? John? Tyrone? It's me. Can you let me in? I'm here. Hello? Hello?

THE PRESENT blinks off and on.

At some point, it stops.

End of play.

Anthem

For G. Though I didn't know it at the time.

CHARACTERS

ANNELIE

A YOUNG WOMAN

A WOMAN FROM OUT OF NOWHERE

DAVE

SCENE

The play takes place in the space. ANNELIE has a suitcase. The suitcase should be beautiful. It should appear to have been many places. The same may be said for ANNELIE.

ANNELIE: I'm just visiting here.

I say that everywhere I go and it's true.

I've lived in fifteen different cities over the last twelve years.

And I've loved them all!

I can do my job from anywhere. I work for a company in Japan. It's actually. It's a French company owned by an Argentinean businessman, but it's run out of Japan and we make lingerie. Actually. I make blindfolds. But it's considered, it is considered to be a lingerie company and they do make lingerie. Some people do. They make night-gowns and underclothes for women. I'm a kind of a— freelancer. I make these blindfolds. For people to wear while they're having sex.

I got the job through a friend of mine. A woman I met a long time ago when I was living in Aarhus. She's one of the designers. She designs the brassieres and when I told her that I had started making these blindfolds she sug-gested that I get in touch with her boss, who is the buyer, because she thought he'd be interested in them. And she was right!

It was a crazy coincidence too because the buyer, he turned out to be this guy who used to play rugby with my brother in college. When I was sixteen, I went to visit my brother at college and I went to one of his rugby games and it was the most violent thing I have ever seen.

I know there are more violent things going on all over the world than rugby, but I have never seen any of that up close. And I don't understand very much about all of that even though I try to understand it sometimes but I usually get confused, and overwhelmed, with useless feelings, and then that's when I usually pack my suitcase and move away somewhere. So that I can feel like I am doing something you know? Even if it isn't something of value.

My friend Rachel she says that I'm doing something of value by making these blindfolds. I'm not sure I agree with her, but sometimes I wonder if there might be something to it. Because a lot of people are buying them. I don't think I'm bragging by telling you that. I just think it's interesting that so many people apparently don't want to see the faces of the people they're having sex with. Unless they aren't actually buying them to wear while they're having sex but are using them for something else, which—Well I wonder what that would be but. It's none of my business I guess, and certainly anyway entirely it's their prerogative.

But anyway at this rugby game I remember it was horrible because one of the players on my brother's team got caught up in this kind of—*pile* that the players make on top of the—*ball* or whatever. And when he came *out* of the pile I remember that his face was a completely different shape from what it had been when he went in. I'd never seen anything like it. I didn't know it was possible for someone's facial features to be completely rearranged like that. It was shocking. He looked like a—like some kind of a—Picasso. But with dirt, and blood, and mud all over him.

I asked the buyer, when I met him for the first time, his name is Williams and when we met he told me that he'd gone to college with a guy who had my same last name. Which is kind of unusual you know? And so anyway I asked Williams, when we figured out that he had indeed gone to college with my brother, I asked him if he'd been at that rugby game, and he told me that he'd not only been there, but that he'd actually been in the pile with that guy. He was on the team! Williams was. And he told me that the guy with the unfortunate face was called Threadgill, and that Threadgill was a friend of his, and that they would still get together sometimes when Williams was in the States. Williams told me that Threadgill lives in the South now, somewhere in Georgia, and I guess he likes it down there, likes the people or. The weather and that kind of stuff.

Anyway it turns out that Threadgill's face apparently has never been the same. And that people actually call him Pablo now. As a nickname. Because of the Picasso thing. So I guess I wasn't the only one clever enough to make that association.

I started making the blindfolds a couple of years ago. Because my friend Genvieve told me she thought we should start writing erotica. She said there was no good erotica out there and she thought we should start writing some.

So I started writing some. Because I wasn't doing anything else right then. Mostly only inventing recipes for parsley sandwiches and pretending to take care of my imaginary children.

I had always wanted to have children but a couple of years ago I realized that I'm probably not going to have any, and also that probably maybe I shouldn't have any given the kind of person that I am and also the kind of direction that the world is taking and all that. But I made up a couple of kids. And a husband for myself. Who was Scandinavian. Because I love the Scandinavians! And I would just spend most of my time, I was unemployed then so I would spend most of my time making up recipes for the parsley that was growing wild in my yard, and making up games and stories for my imaginary children Max and Franz.

That's right. Max. And Franz.

Max was a couple of years older than Franz, and she was imaginative and obstinate and liked to play a horrible music on the pots and pans, which I was always having to take away from her and put back into the imaginary cabinets. And every day I would complain to my imaginary husband, Nigel, I called him Nigel, that we needed to move the linens to the lower closets, where Max could reach, and the pots and pans to the upper cabinets where she couldn't, because her banging was driving me crazy and I thought she could maybe make some nice soft sounds with the pillowcases and dishtowels. Nigel would always imaginarily say that he would get to it. "I'll get to it," he'd say, and then we'd have something parsley for dinner.

Franz, the boy, was younger and more quiet and all he loved to do was play with trucks. And his first words were, "These are my woods." Because in my mind, we lived at the foot of a beautiful woods where he would wander off and play all day and never meet any danger. He didn't talk for a long time because originally I taught him sign language, which is supposed to help with the frustration of children who don't have verbal language capacities yet but who know what they want and so if you can give them a sign for it then they are able to communicate things like "tired" and "hungry" and "nightmare" and this sort of thing. *(She does the sign for each of these words as she says them.)*

But when Genvieve suggested that we start writing erotica, I abandoned my imaginary family and started making up these stories. It was kind of a relief actually because— I don't think I was a very good mother. Or wife. Although I do think some of my parsley recipes are pretty good. But anyway I started writing these short erotic stories and I have to say I really liked doing it! It was great to actually think about what is erotic because... So many things, you know? So many things...

So I got really into it and I wrote this whole cycle of stories that were inspired by important periods and events in world history. *Ice Age. Man on the Moon. The World is Not*

Flat! Panama. (That one was a little depressing. Sexy. But kind of a downer.) Anyway Genvieve really liked them and she gave them to a friend of hers, Tobias, a diamond collector who lives up on a mountain about an hour from here, and he liked them too. He sent me a postcard once that said *I like your erotica* on it, and then he also sent me the name and number of a publisher he knew in the city. A Mr. Nigel (believe it or not) Areopagitica at Euphemiracle Publishing, Inc.

I made an appointment and I brought him my stories and I told him if he liked them I would let him publish them. He says, "What if I don't like them?" and I say, "Well I won't let you publish them then," which he thought was really funny. But I wasn't joking.

I excused myself to the restroom while he looked over some of my writing.

I think the only one he read was *Dust Bowl*. Which wasn't the strongest one of them I don't mind telling you. But when I came back from the ladies' Mr. Areopagitica told me that my stories were horrible but he thought I had a great ass, and would I be interested in going out to dinner with him some night.

I pretended to be offended at first, but after a couple of minutes, we made a date for that Friday.

As I was leaving, Mr. Areopagitica told me that if I wanted to write sexy stories, I should put some blindfolds in them. "Blindfolds are sexy," he said. "That's what your stories need. A little kink. See you on Friday," he said. And I left.

A YOUNG WOMAN bursts in.

YOUNG WOMAN: I heard you saw an angel!

ANNELIE: What?

YOUNG WOMAN: I heard you saw an angel! I heard you saw an angel!

A WOMAN FROM OUT OF NOWHERE: Oh no.

ANNELIE: No, I don't. Think so. No I. Not that I know of.

WOMAN FROM NOWHERE: *(reluctantly)* That was me.

WOMAN FROM NOWHERE: *(a little less reluctantly)* I think that was me.

THE YOUNG WOMAN: Where did you see it?

WOMAN FROM NOWHERE: The other day.

THE YOUNG WOMAN: Was it a girl angel or a boy angel?

WOMAN FROM NOWHERE: It was a woman.

THE YOUNG WOMAN: How old was it? Did it kiss you?

WOMAN FROM NOWHERE: Well I can—Tell you about it if you want but. Maybe we should go in the other room.

YOUNG WOMAN: OK. Yes! Let's go in the other room. I want to hear all about it. I want to hear all about it!

The YOUNG WOMAN and THE WOMAN FROM NOWHERE go in the other room. As they're going:

WOMAN FROM NOWHERE: *(to ANNELIE)* I'm sorry.

ANNELIE doesn't mind. She watches them go.

YOUNG WOMAN: When did it happen?

WOMAN FROM NOWHERE: The other day. I saw her down by the Catherine Slip.

YOUNG WOMAN: Was she old or young?

WOMAN FROM NOWHERE: She was about my age. She was holding up a big fish. A trout I think. I think she was in a fishing contest.

YOUNG WOMAN: Did she win?

WOMAN FROM NOWHERE: I'm pretty sure she did. It was a really big fish.

They're gone.

ANNELIE: So I don't know what it was about Nigel Areopagitica saying that thing about blindfolds being sexy, but I fixated on it for some reason. But instead of putting blindfolds into my stories I stopped writing the stories altogether and started making these blindfolds out of these old handkerchiefs I have that used to belong to my grandmother. I was going to make a quilt out of them and I had started sewing little phrases onto each one, like little facts from my grandmother's life. Her birthday and her maiden name, the hospital where she was born and different addresses she lived at. And funny things she was fond of saying like—

Well I can't remember any of them right now but anyway when I went home that day from my meeting with Nigel I stitched a few of my grandmother's handkerchiefs together to make a blindfold for him and then I stitched also the words "don't look at me" onto it. And I gave it to him on Friday when we went out for our date.

I gave it to him after we ordered our dessert. He had the honey pine nut tart and I had the lemon panna cotta.

He unwrapped the blindfold. I didn't put it in a box or anything. I didn't want it to seem like too much of a big deal. But I had wrapped it up in some tissue paper so it wouldn't get messed up. And he unwrapped it, and when he figured out what it was it really made him laugh out loud. I wasn't expecting that but I thought it was kind of great you know. Because having a sense of humor is really—Or at least—Not having a sense of humor is certainly anyway very *not* sexy so. I thought the inverse might also be true.

Anyway when he was done laughing I said, "I made that for you, Nigel." And then he just looked at me for a long time. And finally he said, "I really like the way you say my name." And then he asked me to say it again.

So I said it again and then he said, "You say my name like you've been saying it for a hundred years."

"Yes well, I did have an imaginary husband named Nigel for quite some time. We had two imaginary kids together. But we've recently split."

No. *(She didn't say that.)*

But we did go home together that night. And we did a lot of crazy things. I didn't feel comfortable using the blindfold though because it kept making me think about my grandmother. Plus Nigel said blindfolds should be black. Or mostly black. So that was when I started making the ones that I sell now to the French-Argentinean-Japanese lingerie company! Those are all black. But I still sew little phrases onto them. But now I stitch them into the insides, into the lining in between the front piece and the back piece where the people who wear them won't know they're there. Now sometimes I sew in things from my own life. Like dates when something significant has happened to me. Or sometimes maybe something someone has said. When I don't have anything from my own life to sew in there, sometimes I'll put in a headline from one of the daily newspapers. Or if I get one of those postcards in the mail of a child who's gone missing, sometimes I will put their name in there and the amount of time they've been gone. I don't know if that's right or not. To do that. But I'm just. Yeah anyway...

The YOUNG WOMAN and the WOMAN FROM NOWHERE laugh in the other room. They laugh for a long time.

ANNELIE listens.

DAVE appears toward the end of the laughing.

DAVE: Hey have you seen Angie?

ANNELIE: Unh unh. I haven't.

DAVE: …Damn.

DAVE stands there.

Then leaves.

ANNELIE: But yeah. I have so many regrets. So many. There are just. So many things I would have done differently.

THE YOUNG WOMAN: *(from the other room)* Oh my god no. Don't tell me that. I don't want to know something like that. It's too much. It's too far.

ANNELIE: Like remember that time we were walking in the freezing cold through the ghetto watching the children ice skate down the frozen streets on—on hand-me-down skates they got from that misguided relief program? "If they're having fun, maybe they won't notice they're hungry!" That was the last mayor's big plan, that was the big idea of his administration. Old boots made into ice skates with butter knives and hot glue for the poor children. But anyway remember how that one kid, armed with a zipgun and shaking that handful of homemade aluminum foil bullets in his hand like they were—dice or—no something more ominous—But remember how he stopped where I was stopped because my toes were literally frozen in my shoes? I mean literally. There was actual ice forming between my toes and remember how you said, "You got to keep them moving if you want to keep them from freezing!" So I was taking off my shoe and trying to wiggle some of the ice from my toes and that kid, with the bullets, he stopped in front of me and I thought he was going to hurt me but then he just said, he just said, "Are you lost?"

She gets a little sad and upset thinking about this.

Are you lost.

She shakes her head.

I'm sorry. I don't know.

You want to see something?

She opens her suitcase and takes out a mask. It's a half-mask made of felt and decorated with glitter. It's a handmade kitten mask, with whiskers, and little ears sewn onto the top. She shows it to the audience.

This is a prototype.

She puts it on.

What do you think?

I like it.

Meow.

Meowmeow.

. . .

She pushes the kitten mask up onto her forehead.

But all that was a long time ago I guess.

Last night I dreamed that there were
flowers
growing out of my eyes.
Purple flowers, like
irises. Or crocuses.
They were growing out of my tear ducts.
I kept trying to break them off but then they would just
grow back immediately.
It was a nightmare. *(She does the sign for the word night-mare.)*

I asked Williams recently for Threadgill's address. Pablo?
Picasso? I didn't really know what I wanted it for but he
sent it to me yesterday on a post-it note stuck to my pay-
check for this period.

He lives on the Old Post Road. In Madison, Georgia,
30650.

That sounds nice. Doesn't it?

So now I'm thinking I might go down there. I'm thinking
I might go down there and look him up.

THE YOUNG WOMAN and the WOMAN FROM NOWHERE talk in the other room about the angel.

WOMAN FROM NOWHERE: And then she told me that

I would live a long time.

That I would live a long time and that

One day

My husband would go to work

And I said, "I don't have a husband."

And she said

One day

Your husband will go to work in the morning

And you will say good-bye to him on the steps of your house

And later in the day

You will go out into your yard

To pick plums.

Under the plum tree in your yard

In a nice light on a nice day

Your heart—

And then I didn't hear what she said after that. It got jumbled for a minute like it was only static coming out of her mouth.

A strange sound and light. A mysterious flash of something like wings.

But then in the end she said
The coroner's report
will state that you didn't suffer.

That you didn't suffer.

The sound and light and continue. And finally come to an end.

End of Play.

Kristen Kosmas is an American playwright and performer. Her plays and solo performances have been produced in Seattle, Austin, Boston, Chicago, and in New York City at numerous venues including the Prelude festival, Performance Space 122, The Poetry Project, Dixon Place, Little Theater, Barbès, and the Ontological/Hysteric Downstairs Series. She has had new works commissioned by Performance Space 122, The Theatre of a Two-Headed Calf, Seattle University's SITE Specific, Dixon Place, and the New City Theater in Seattle. Her play *Hello Failure* was published by Ugly Duckling Presse; her multi-voice performance text *This From Cloudland* appears in *PLAY A Journal of Plays*. Other plays and performance texts include *Bad Sailors*, *H.*, *Chapter of Accidents*, *H-O-R-S-E*, and *Palomino*. Kosmas is the writer/performer of four critically acclaimed solo shows: *Blah Blah Fuckin Blah, Again* (Top Ten Great Theater Events of the Decade, Seattle Stranger), *Slip* (Seattle Times Best Solo Show of the Year, 1996), and *The Scandal!* (Best Short Script nominee, New York Independent Theater Awards, 2009). As an actor, Kristen has appeared in many notable new plays including *Potatoes of August* by Sibyl Kempson, *Mark Smith* by Kate Ryan, *ASTRS* and *Some Things Cease* by Karinne Keithley, *The Internationalist* by Anne Washburn, *Producers of Fiction* by Jim Strahs, *Playstation Levels 1-4* by Judy Elkan, *The Florida Project* by Tory Vazquez, and *Hurricane* by Erin Cressida Wilson. Kosmas is a founding member of the OBIE Award winning performance series Little Theater; the Brooklyn-based experimental writer's collective Machiqq/The Ladies' Auxiliary Playwriting Team; and The Twenty-Five Cent Opera of San Francisco, a monthly event for the enactment of texts and theatricals.

Thank you Chris Speed first and foremost. Thank you so much also to Kip Fagan and the many, many actors, playwrights, artists, and other geniuses who appeared at one time or another in these plays: Mary Q. Archias, Jane Beachy, Deron Bos, Tom Bradshaw, Chris Caniglia, Lisa D'Amour, Mary Ewold, Elena Ewold-Kazanjian, Alissa Ford, Forrest Gillespie, Lula Graves, Ann Marie Healy, Rachel Hoeffel, Haley Hughes, Jesse Karch, John Kazanjian, Elizabeth Kenny, Horam Kim, Tina Kunz, Denver Latimer, Elizabeth Latimer, Tyler Nolan, Josh Olivera, Dana Olson, Estee Pierce, Julia Pearlstein, Kate Ryan, Jenny Schwartz, Normandy Sherwood, Heidi Schreck, Elizabeth Taylor, and Valerie Trucchia. Very special thanks also to the students at Whitman College who gave their time and attention to this project, particularly Elizabeth Daviess, Michaela Gianotti, Taia Handlin, Florence LeBas, Henry Nolan, Theo Pratt, Zoe Randol, and Alexandra Shaffer. Thank you Tonic. Thank you Barbès. Thank you New City.

The Mayor of Baltimore and *Anthem* were commissioned by and presented at Dixon Place in February 2006, with support from the New York State Council on the Arts – a state agency, The Dramatists Guild Fund, Jerome Foundation, Andrew W. Mellon Foundation, and The Peg Santvoord Foundation.

Book design and cover images: Karinne Keithley Syers

Printed on recycled paper.

53rd State Press publishes new writing for performance. It was founded in 2007 by Karinne Keithley, is incorporated in the state of Illinois, and is co-edited by Karinne Keithley Syers and Antje Oegel.

For more information or to order books, visit 53rdstatepress.org.

53SP 01   The Book of the Dog
53SP 02   Joyce Cho Plays
53SP 03   Nature Theater of Oklahoma's No Dice
53SP 04   Nature Theater of Oklahoma's Rambo Solo
53SP 05   When You Rise Up
53SP 06   Montgomery Park, or Opulence
53SP 07   Crime or Emergency
53SP 08   Off the Hozzle
53SP 09   A Map of Virtue and Black Cat Lost
53SP 10   Pig Iron: Three Plays
53SP 11   The Mayor of Baltimore and Anthem

Forthcoming in 2012-13: plays by Erik Ehn, Sibyl Kempson and Big Dance Theater.